STATE PROFILES

KENTUCKY

BY ALICIA Z. KLEPEIS

BLASTOFF! DISCOVERY

BELLWETHER MEDIA • MINNEAPOLIS, MN

Blastoff! Discovery launches a new mission: reading to learn. Filled with facts and features, each book offers you an exciting new world to explore!

BLASTOFF! UNIVERSE

BLASTOFF! Beginners — GRADE K

BLASTOFF! READERS — GRADES 1-3

BLASTOFF! DISCOVERY — GRADE 4

This edition first published in 2022 by Bellwether Media, Inc.

No part of this publication may be reproduced in whole or in part without written permission of the publisher.
For information regarding permission, write to Bellwether Media, Inc., Attention: Permissions Department,
6012 Blue Circle Drive, Minnetonka, MN 55343.

Library of Congress Cataloging-in-Publication Data

Names: Klepeis, Alicia, 1971- author.
Title: Kentucky / by Alicia Z. Klepeis.
Description: Minneapolis, MN : Bellwether Media, Inc., 2022. |
   Series: Blastoff! Discovery: State profiles | Includes bibliographical
   references and index. | Audience: Ages 7-13 | Audience: Grades 4-6 |
   Summary: "Engaging images accompany information about Kentucky.
   The combination of high-interest subject matter and narrative text is
   intended for students in grades 3 through 8"– Provided by publisher.
Identifiers: LCCN 2021019681 (print) | LCCN 2021019682 (ebook) |
   ISBN 9781644873885 (library binding) | ISBN 9781648341656 (ebook)
Subjects: LCSH: Kentucky–Juvenile literature.
Classification: LCC F451.3 .K47 2022 (print) | LCC F451.3 (ebook) |
   DDC 976.9–dc23
LC record available at https://lccn.loc.gov/2021019681
LC ebook record available at https://lccn.loc.gov/2021019682

Editor: Kate Moening   Designer: Jeffrey Kollock

Printed in the United States of America, North Mankato, MN.

TABLE OF CONTENTS

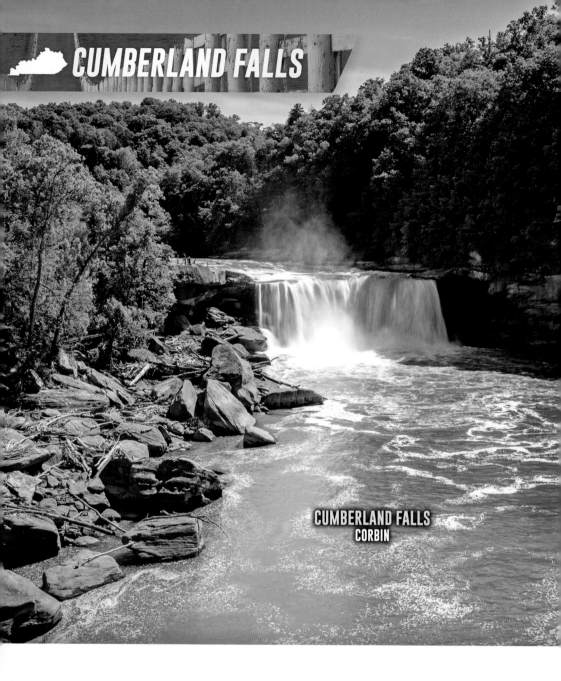

CUMBERLAND FALLS
CORBIN

It is a muggy summer day at Cumberland Falls State Resort Park. A family quickly sets up their tent. They head down to the Cumberland River for a guided rafting trip. Bright yellow goldfinches fly along the shore as the river tosses the raft about.

ABRAHAM LINCOLN BIRTHPLACE NATIONAL HISTORICAL PARK

KENTUCKY HORSE PARK

LAND BETWEEN THE LAKES

RED RIVER GORGE

In the late afternoon, the family goes for a horseback ride through the forest. After dinner by the campfire, they head to Cumberland Falls. The night is clear. The only sound is the rush of the falls. Suddenly, a **moonbow** appears. Its colors brighten the night sky. Welcome to Kentucky!

Kentucky is in the eastern and central United States. It covers 40,408 square miles (104,656 square kilometers). The state capital, Frankfort, is in northern Kentucky. The biggest city, Louisville, is also in northern Kentucky. It lies on the Ohio River.

Rivers form most of Kentucky's borders. The mighty Mississippi River flows between Kentucky and its southwestern neighbor, Missouri. To the north, the Ohio River separates Kentucky from Illinois, Indiana, and Ohio. To the northeast, the Big Sandy River forms the border with West Virginia. Virginia sits to Kentucky's southeast. Tennessee lies south of Kentucky.

ILLINOIS

MISSOURI

KENTUCKY LAKE

MISSISSIPPI RIVER

INDIANA

OHIO

N
W+E
S

OHIO
RIVER

FRANKFORT

★

BIG SANDY
RIVER —

LOUISVILLE

LEXINGTON

WEST
VIRGINIA —

KENTUCKY

VIRGINIA

BOWLING GREEN

TENNESSEE

ONE LARGE LAKE

Kentucky Lake is the state's biggest lake. Located in southwestern Kentucky, this manmade lake is 184 miles (296 kilometers) long. It has over 2,300 miles (3,701 kilometers) of shoreline.

DANIEL BOONE

BOONESBOROUGH

Daniel Boone was one of Kentucky's most famous early settlers. In 1775, he helped found the community of Boonesborough on the Kentucky River. Today the site is part of Fort Boonesborough State Park.

The first people came to what is now Kentucky at least 14,000 years ago. These early residents may have followed mammoths and other big game animals. They were **ancestors** of Native American peoples such as the Shawnee, Cherokee, Yuchi, and Chickasaw.

French and Spanish explorers arrived in the area in the 1600s. The first European **settlements** were built during the 1770s. Early settlers were often hunters, merchants, or farmers. At first, Kentucky was part of Virginia. It became its own state in 1792. Kentucky was the 15th state.

NATIVE PEOPLES OF KENTUCKY

The Cherokee, Shawnee, Chickasaw, and Yuchi were Kentucky's most recent Native American residents before European settlement. There are no government-recognized Native American tribes in Kentucky today.

CHEROKEE

- Original lands in southeastern Kentucky
- Descendants largely in the Cherokee Nation of Oklahoma
- Also called Keetoowah, Tsalagi, and Aniyunwiya

SHAWNEE

- Original lands across central, northern, and northeastern Kentucky
- Descendants largely in Oklahoma
- A group of five separate nations: Chalahgawtha, Mekoche, Kispoko, Pekowi, and Hathawekela

YUCHI

- Original lands in southeastern Kentucky
- Some descendants are part of the Muscogee Nation in Oklahoma
- Also called Tsoyaha

CHICKASAW

- Original lands in western Kentucky
- Descendants largely in the Chickasaw Nation in Oklahoma

Kentucky's landscape is highest in the east. This area of the Appalachian Mountains includes Pine Mountain and the Cumberland Range. Extending west from these mountains is a region called the Interior Low **Plateaus**. This section of Kentucky includes the Bluegrass region, known for its lush grass. Western Kentucky has flat **plains** with good soil for farming. Bald cypress swamps are also found there.

N
W + E
S

■ BLUEGRASS REGION
■ APPALACHIAN MOUNTAINS

PINE MOUNTAIN
APPALACHIAN MOUNTAINS

MAMMOTH CAVE

Located beneath central Kentucky, Mammoth Cave is the world's longest cave system. It has more than 400 miles (644 kilometers) of caves. Unusual animals such as cave crayfish and eyeless fish live in the caves.

MAMMOTH CAVE

SPRING
HIGH: 66°F (19°C)
LOW: 46°F (8°C)

SUMMER
HIGH: 87°F (31°C)
LOW: 66°F (19°C)

FALL
HIGH: 68°F (20°C)
LOW: 47°F (8°C)

WINTER
HIGH: 44°F (7°C)
LOW: 27°F (-3°C)

°F = degrees Fahrenheit
°C = degrees Celsius

Kentucky has a **continental** climate. Winters are cool and summers are warm. Rain falls all year long, especially in southern Kentucky. Natural disasters include floods, landslides, and tornadoes.

A wide variety of wildlife lives in Kentucky. The state's many waterways are home to over 200 kinds of fish. They include bluegills, bass, and catfish. River otters and minks dive down in search of crayfish or frogs to eat.

Double-crested cormorants and great blue herons build nests and raise their chicks in Kentucky's wetlands. Kentucky warblers fly across the state. Golden mice try to avoid becoming meals for kingsnakes in Kentucky's woodlands. Two-lined salamanders search for worms and insects among the leaves. Black bears wander the Appalachian forests searching for berries.

RIVER OTTERS

DOUBLE-CRESTED CORMORANTS

BLACK KINGSNAKE

BLACK BEAR

SOUTHERN TWO-LINED SALAMANDER

AMERICAN MINK

Life Span: 10 years
Status: least concern

American mink range = ◼

LEAST CONCERN	NEAR THREATENED	VULNERABLE	ENDANGERED	CRITICALLY ENDANGERED	EXTINCT IN THE WILD	EXTINCT
▲						

Kentucky is home to more than 4.5 million people. More than half of Kentuckians live in **urban** areas. The state's biggest city is Louisville, with over 600,000 residents. Lexington is its second-largest city.

THE GOLDEN TRIANGLE

The area between Louisville, Lexington, and the section of northern Kentucky containing Newport and Covington is called the Golden Triangle. Over half of the state's population lives there. It is very important to Kentucky's economy.

LEXINGTON

FAMOUS KENTUCKIAN

Name: Muhammad Ali
Born: January 17, 1942
Died: June 3, 2016
Hometown: Louisville, Kentucky
Famous For: One of the greatest boxers of all time, an Olympic gold medalist, and the first three-time heavyweight champion, as well as a leader in the civil rights movement and a United Nations Messenger of Peace

The majority of Kentuckians have European backgrounds. Many have ancestors from Germany, England, or Ireland. Black or African American Kentuckians make up the second-biggest group. The Hispanic population in Kentucky has been growing quickly in the past decade. Native Americans make up a very small number of Kentuckians. The population of immigrants in Kentucky is increasing. Many recent arrivals come from Mexico, India, Cuba, and China.

An American military leader named George Rogers Clark founded Louisville in 1778. The city's location on the Ohio River quickly made it an important trade center. During the 20th century, many factories opened. They produced goods including cars, paint, and baseball bats.

KENTUCKY'S CHALLENGE: CLEAN DRINKING WATER

Kentucky's drinking water has been getting worse in some places, including Louisville. This happens when pollution gets into water supplies. This can cause serious health problems for people. Animals may also die out in areas without clean water.

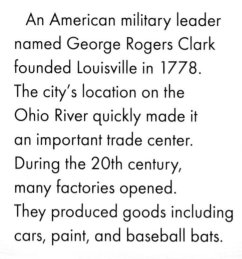

CUBAN COMMUNITY

People from Cuba make up the fastest-growing group of immigrants in Louisville. The city has Cuban restaurants, grocery stores, and many other Cuban-owned businesses.

LOUISVILLE SLUGGER MUSEUM

Today, **tourism** is an important part of Louisville's economy. People come to learn about the city's history. The Louisville Slugger Museum shares the story of baseball. The famous Kentucky Derby horse race takes place at Churchill Downs. This gives Louisville its nickname of Derby City!

17

THOROUGHBRED HORSES

Kentucky's rich soil is an important **natural resource**. Many early Kentuckians worked as farmers. The state is still a large producer of soybeans, hay, tobacco, and wheat. Kentucky is also the country's biggest breeder of **Thoroughbred** horses. Most Kentuckians today have **service jobs**. Some have jobs in banks or schools. Others work at hotels, restaurants, and museums.

Much of Kentucky's income comes from **manufacturing**. Factories produce cars, trucks, chemicals, and plastics. Coal also earns more than a billion dollars each year.

INVENTED IN KENTUCKY

"HAPPY BIRTHDAY TO YOU" MELODY

Date Invented: 1893
Inventors: Mildred Jane Hill and Patty Smith Hill

DISCO BALL

Date Patented: 1917
Inventor: Louis B. Woeste

LOUISVILLE SLUGGER BAT

Date Invented: 1884
Inventor: John A. "Bud" Hillerich

HOT BROWN

Kentuckians take pride in their local food. Burgoo is a spicy stew. It typically includes pork, beef, or chicken, as well as okra and corn. Fried catfish and barbecue are other popular dishes. Sandwich lovers can enjoy a Hot Brown. This open-faced sandwich has turkey, bacon, and a creamy sauce.

AWESOME AIRHEADS

Each day a factory in Erlanger, Kentucky, makes 3 million fruity Airheads candies. Placed end to end, one year's production would be enough to reach the moon and back two and a half times!

People around the world eat at Kentucky Fried Chicken. This restaurant chain started in Corbin, Kentucky. The state also has its share of special sweet treats. Modjeska is a chewy candy with caramel and marshmallow. Kentucky chess pie has a creamy and sugary filling.

BURGOO

KENTUCKY FRIED CHICKEN

DERBY PIE

8 SERVINGS

Derby Pie was first made at the Melrose Inn in the city of Prospect. It is served at the Kentucky Derby. Have an adult help you make this recipe.

INGREDIENTS

1 cup sugar

4 eggs

1 cup light corn syrup

1/2 cup (1 stick) butter, melted and cooled slightly

1 cup pecans, chopped

3/4 cup semisweet chocolate chips

1 1/4 teaspoons vanilla

1 9-inch unbaked (deep dish) pie shell

DIRECTIONS

1. Preheat the oven to 350 degrees Fahrenheit (177 degrees Celsius).

2. In a large bowl, mix together the sugar, eggs, and corn syrup. Combine until well blended.

3. Add the remaining ingredients into the bowl. Pour into the unbaked pie shell.

4. Bake for 45-50 minutes until the pie looks set. Let cool a bit before eating. Enjoy!

21

KAYAKING

From golfing to hiking, Kentucky offers locals and visitors many fun activities. People kayak, go caving, and bike in Kentucky's 45 state parks. College basketball is also hugely popular. Locals cheer on the Kentucky Wildcats.

Kentucky is famous for **bluegrass** music. It is a mixture of blues, folk, jazz, and gospel music. It has roots in **traditional** music from both the British Isles and parts of Africa. Bluegrass performers often play the banjo, fiddle, and guitar. Kentucky's rich performing arts scene also includes theater and dance.

BLUEGRASS PERFORMANCE

NOTABLE SPORTS TEAM

University of Kentucky Wildcats
Sport: National Collegiate Athletic Association basketball
Started: 1903
Place of Play: Rupp Arena

Kentuckians attend many fun festivals each year. Louisville hosts the Kentucky Derby Festival each spring. Events include live music, the Pegasus Parade, a marathon, and fantastic fireworks displays. Each summer, visitors to the Kentucky State Fair can hear musical performances and go on rides. The World's Championship Horse Show is another State Fair tradition.

In September, Hopkinsville hosts the **Trail of Tears** Intertribal **Pow Wow**. Dance competitions and flute demonstrations celebrate Native American **cultures**. Kentuckians host festivals and celebrate their traditions all year long!

FANTASTIC FOOD FESTIVALS

Kentucky has several barbecue festivals throughout the year. Other food events include the Monroe County Watermelon Festival and the Casey County Apple Festival.

PEGASUS PARADE
KENTUCKY DERBY FESTIVAL

1830

The Indian Removal Act is passed, forcing many Native Americans to leave Kentucky and head west along the Trail of Tears

1600s

Several Spanish and French explorers arrive in what is now Kentucky

1792

Kentucky becomes the 15th state in the U.S.

1770s

Kentucky's first permanent European settlements are founded

1861-1865

The Civil War divides Kentucky, with about 100,000 Kentucky soldiers fighting for the Union and as many as 40,000 fighting for the Confederacy

1936

The U.S. Treasury's gold vault is established at Fort Knox

1983

Martha Layne Collins becomes Kentucky's first woman to be elected governor

1941

Mammoth Cave National Park is established

2019

Kentucky's governor declares a state of emergency after heavy rains cause flooding

1875

The first Kentucky Derby race takes place

KENTUCKY FACTS

Nickname: The Bluegrass State

Motto: United We Stand, Divided We Fall

Date of Statehood: June 1, 1792 (the 15th state)

Capital City: Frankfort ★

Other Major Cities: Louisville, Lexington, Bowling Green

Area: 40,408 square miles (104,656 square kilometers);
Kentucky is the 37th largest state.

Population

4,505,836
(2020)

STATE FLAG

The background of the Kentucky flag is navy blue. In the center is the state seal. It features a statesman and a pioneer. Their interaction is meant to show the state motto of United We Stand, Divided We Fall. Kentucky's motto is also within the seal. Above the seal are the words "Commonweath of Kentucky." Beneath the seal are goldenrod flowers.

INDUSTRY

Main Exports

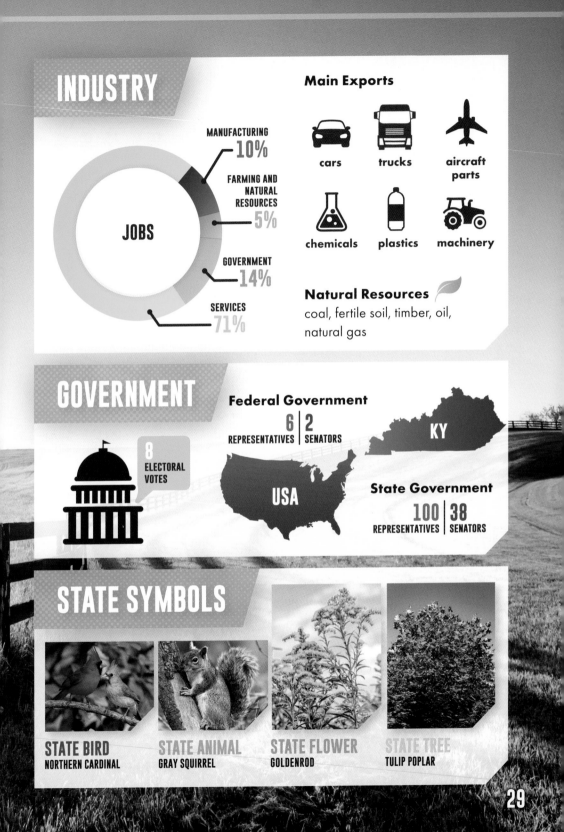

cars

trucks

aircraft parts

chemicals

plastics

machinery

JOBS

MANUFACTURING
10%

FARMING AND NATURAL RESOURCES
5%

GOVERNMENT
14%

SERVICES
71%

Natural Resources
coal, fertile soil, timber, oil, natural gas

GOVERNMENT

Federal Government
6 REPRESENTATIVES | 2 SENATORS

8 ELECTORAL VOTES

KY

USA

State Government
100 REPRESENTATIVES | 38 SENATORS

STATE SYMBOLS

STATE BIRD
NORTHERN CARDINAL

STATE ANIMAL
GRAY SQUIRREL

STATE FLOWER
GOLDENROD

STATE TREE
TULIP POPLAR

29

GLOSSARY

ancestors—relatives who lived long ago

bluegrass—a style of music played on string instruments; bluegrass began in the southern Appalachian region of the United States.

continental—referring to a climate that has hot summers and cold winters, such as those found in central North America and Asia

cultures—beliefs, arts, and ways of life in places or societies

immigrants—people who move to a new country

manufacturing—a field of work in which people use machines to make products

moonbow—a rainbow that is produced by moonlight rather than direct sunlight

natural resource—a material in the earth that is taken out and used to make products or fuel

plains—large areas of flat land

plateaus—areas of flat, raised land

pow wow—a Native American gathering that usually includes dancing

service jobs—jobs that perform tasks for people or businesses

settlements—places where newly arrived people live

Thoroughbred—a breed of fast horses used mainly for racing

tourism—the business of people traveling to visit other places

traditional—related to customs, ideas, or beliefs handed down from one generation to the next

Trail of Tears—the forced relocation of up to 100,000 Native Americans from their homelands to areas farther west in the 1830s; about 15,000 people died on the journey.

urban—related to cities and city life

AT THE LIBRARY

Murray, Julie. *Kentucky*. Minneapolis, Minn.: Abdo Publishing, 2020.

Rajczak, Michael. *Muhammad Ali*. New York, N.Y.: Gareth Stevens, 2021.

Zeiger, Jennifer. *Kentucky*. New York, N.Y.: Children's Press, 2018.

ON THE WEB

FACTSURFER

Factsurfer.com gives you a safe, fun way to find more information.

1. Go to www.factsurfer.com.

2. Enter "Kentucky" into the search box and click 🔍.

3. Select your book cover to see a list of related content.

INDEX